THE LITTLE INSTRUCTION BOOK FOR

Dog Parents

a Hilarious survival guide for dog owners

ILLUSTRATED BY
FIN KENDALL

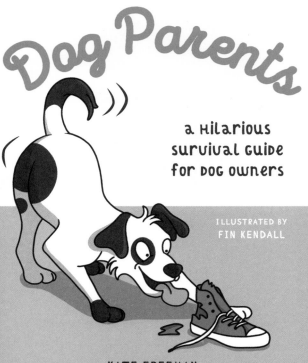

KATE FREEMAN

summersdale

THE LITTLE INSTRUCTION BOOK FOR DOG PARENTS

Text by Lucy York
Illustrations by Fin Kendall

An Hachette UK Company
www.hachette.co.uk

Summersdale Publishers
Part of Octopus Publishing Group Limited
Carmelite House
50 Victoria Embankment
LONDON
EC4Y 0DZ
UK

www.summersdale.com

The authorized representative in the EEA is Hachette Ireland, 8 Castlecourt Centre, Castleknock Road, Castleknock, Dublin 15, D15 YF6A, Ireland.

Printed and bound in Poland

ISBN: 978-1-83799-364-2

This FSC® label means that materials used for the product have been responsibly sourced

MIX
Paper | Supporting responsible forestry
FSC® C018236

Substantial discounts on bulk quantities of Summersdale books are available to corporations, professional associations and other organizations. For details contact general enquiries: telephone: +44 (0) 1243 771107 or email: enquiries@summersdale.com.

Introduction

Congratulations, you're a dog parent!

Make no mistake, it's a full-time pursuit. Your dog is there to wake you in the morning, at your side in the bathroom, by your feet while you eat, getting *under* your feet most of the day… but who can complain when they're such a cutie-patootie little snuggle-woof?

Whether you are a newbie or an old hand at the role, this no-nonsense handbook will guide you through the joys, surprises and occasional downright silliness of sharing your home with a canine.

After all, being a dog parent is not a choice, but a lifestyle!

Wave goodbye to
personal space.

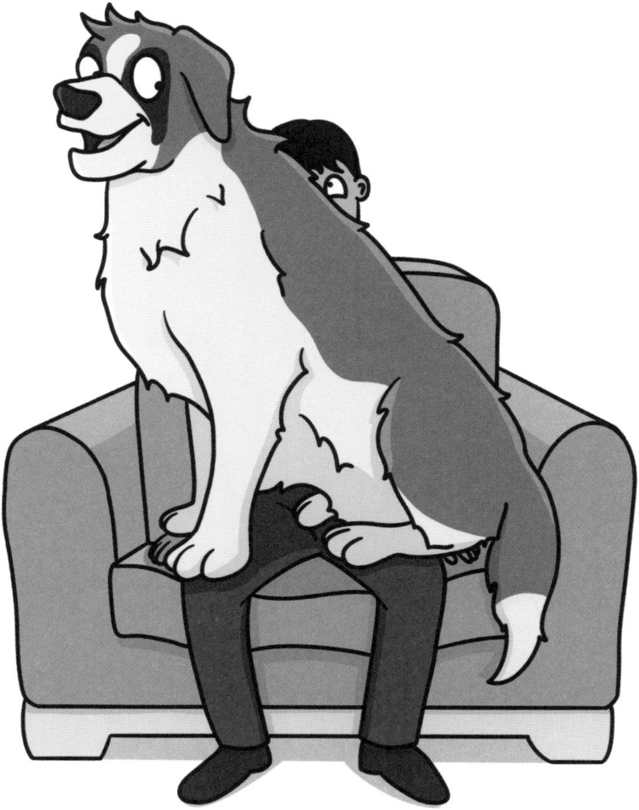

Your dog comes with an in-built floor-cleaning function. Situate near a small child to activate.

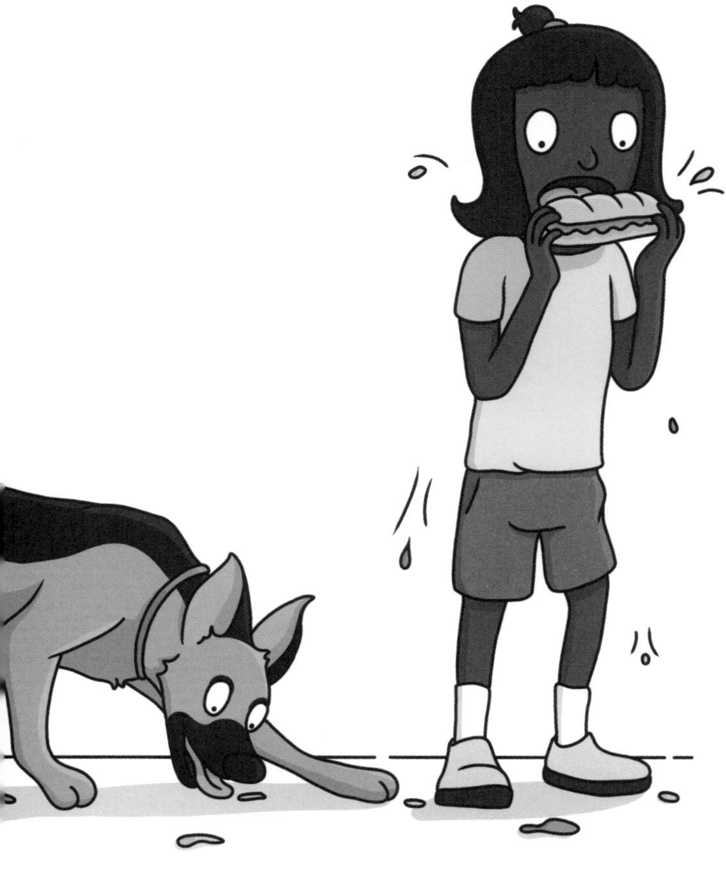

Always call your dog back
to you immediately if you
see them approaching a body
of water. But know that
this is completely futile.

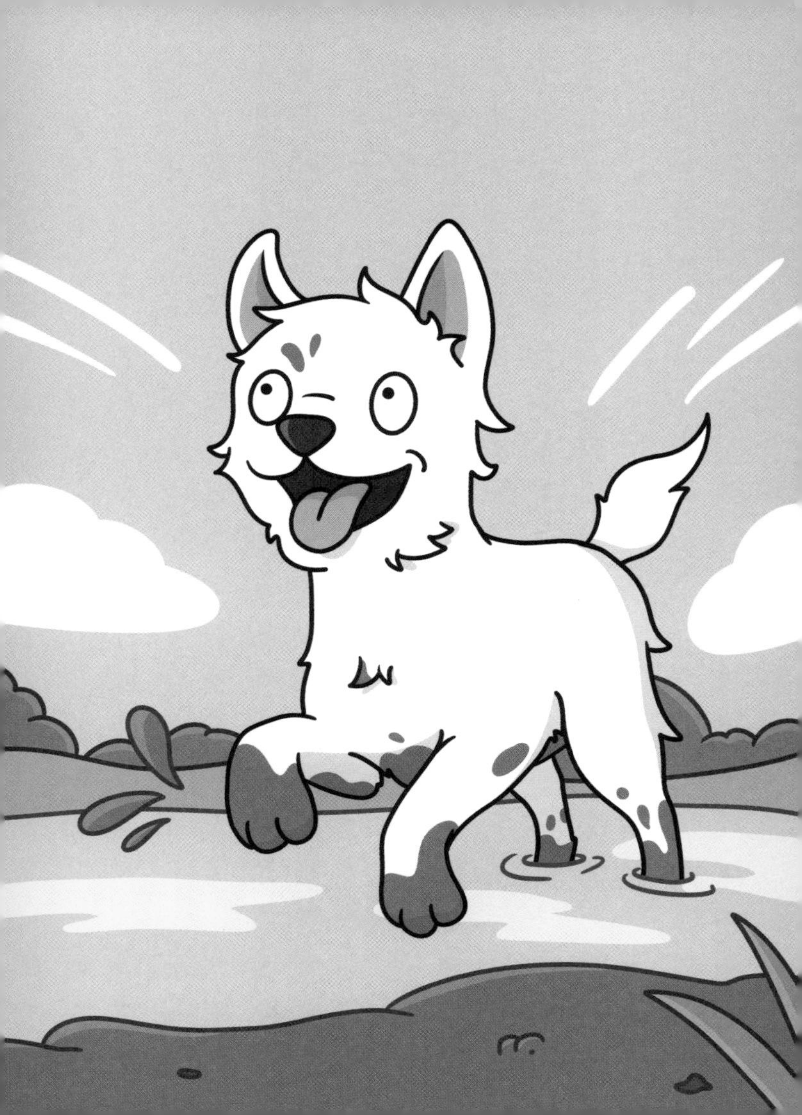

The canine race will
never relent in its quest
to eliminate the number
one threat to humanity.

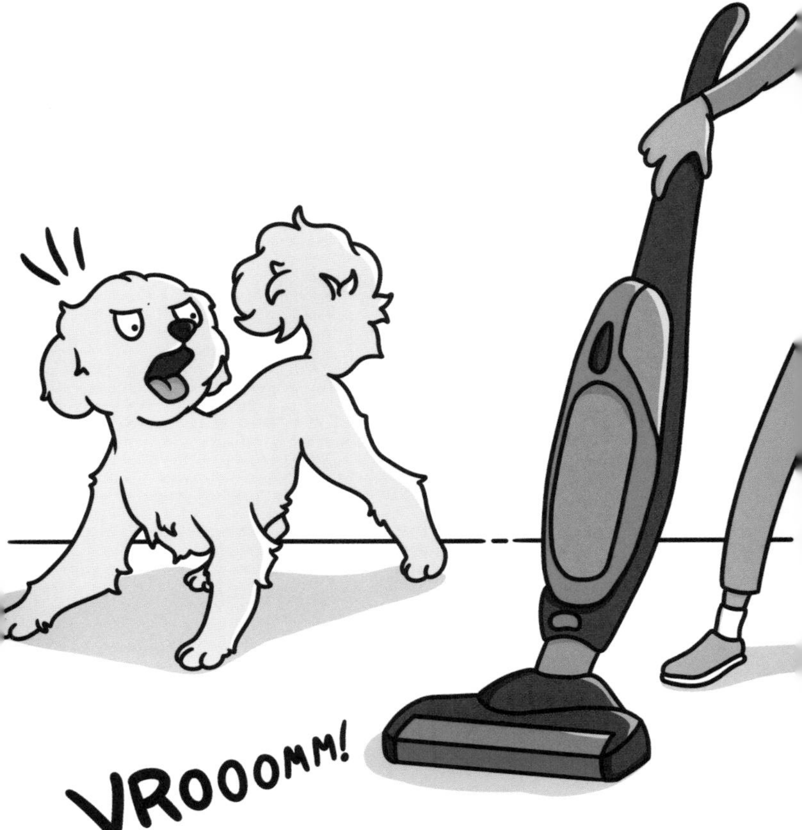
VROOOMM!

Dogs are easily
pleased — especially when
it comes to snacks.

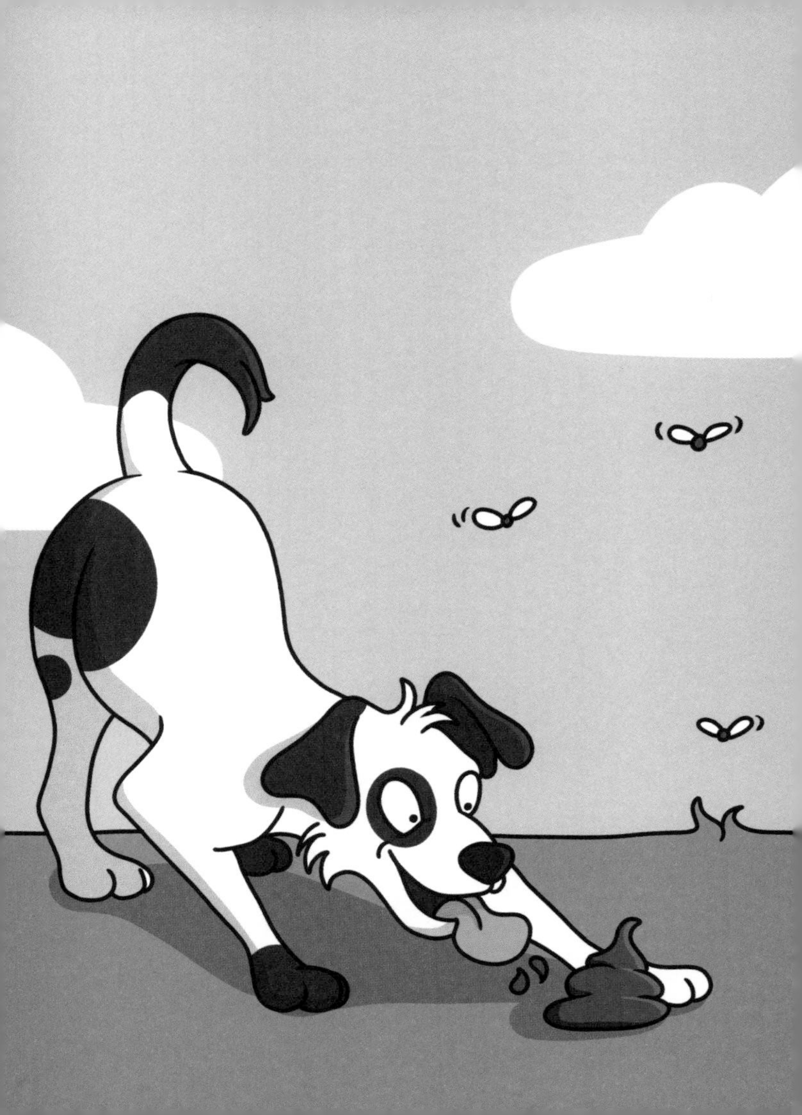

Chewing is an important part of every dog's oral hygiene routine.

Invest in extra cloud storage. You'll need it for all the photos you'll be taking of your pooch.

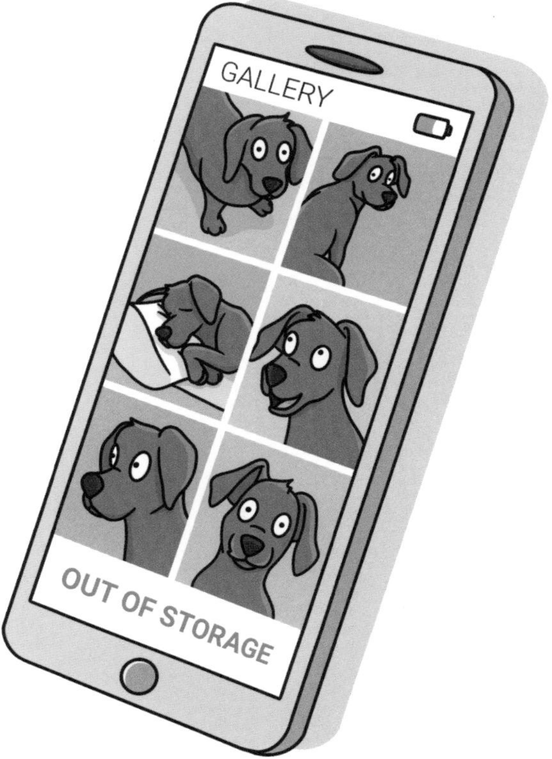
GALLERY
OUT OF STORAGE

Never look down when eating. Who could resist those smoochy-woochy puppy dog eyes?

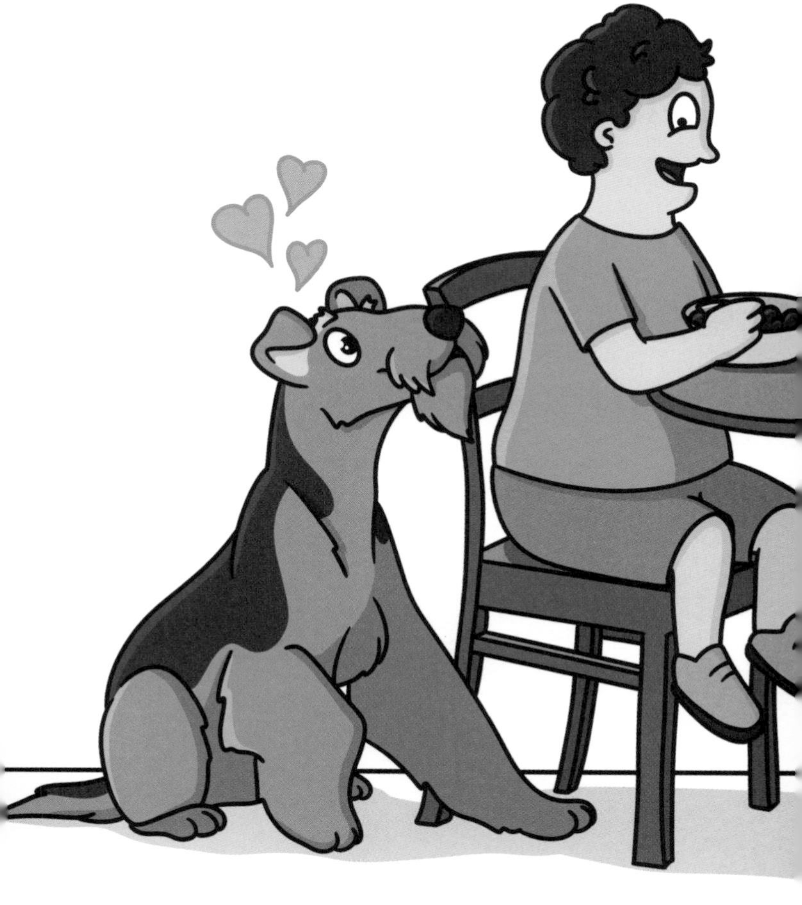

Dogs are very clean animals. They are particularly meticulous when it comes to post-toilet hygiene.

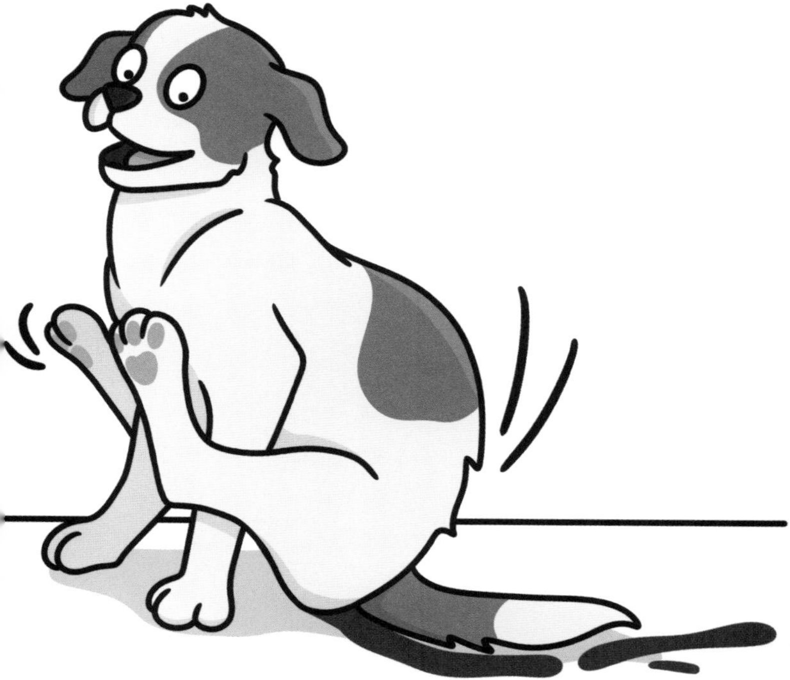

Cuddles may be requested by means of a subtle gesture. It is considered very impolite to decline.

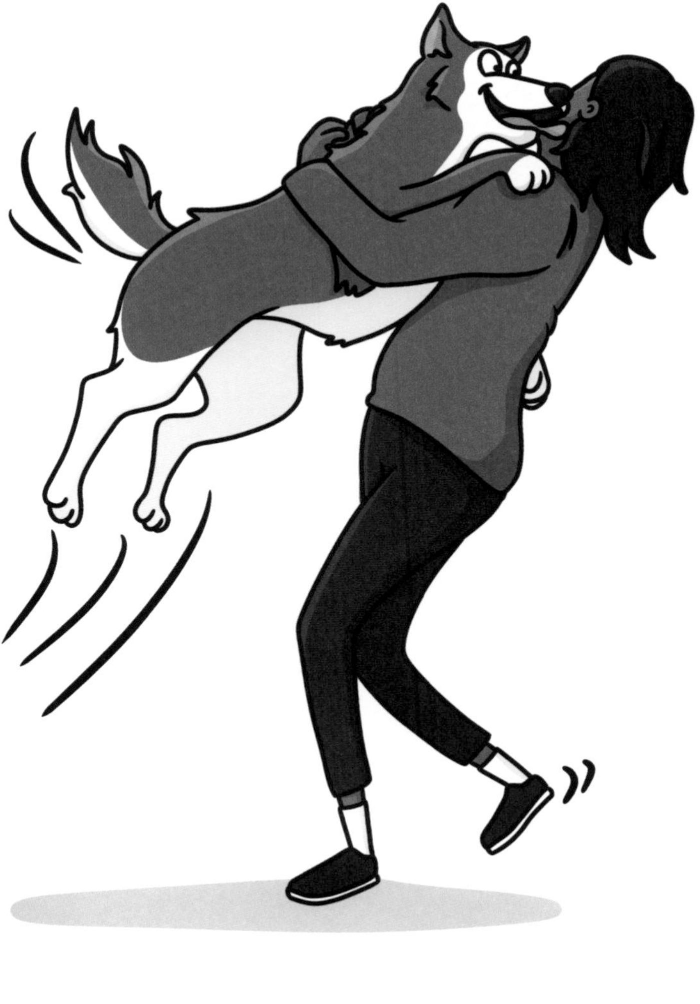

Guess what? Your sofa now doubles up as a handy storage area!

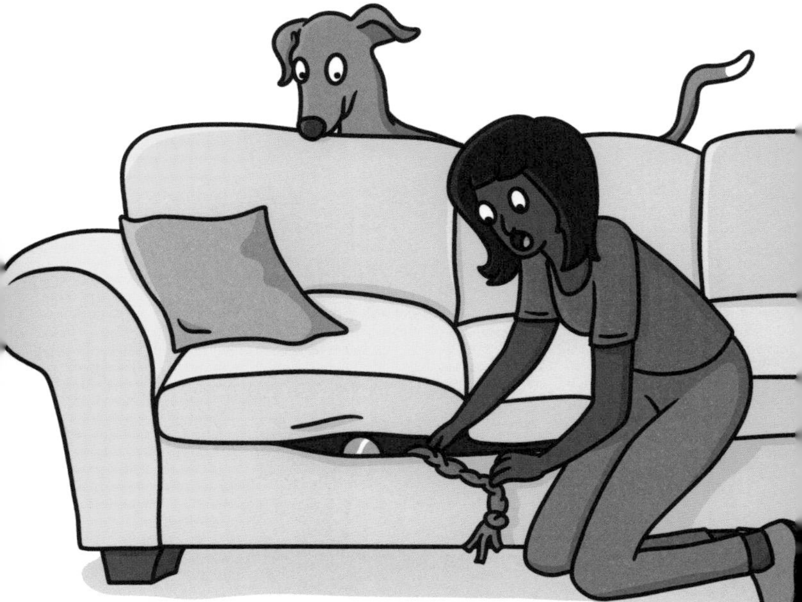

Dogs are very
offended by farts.
Especially their own.

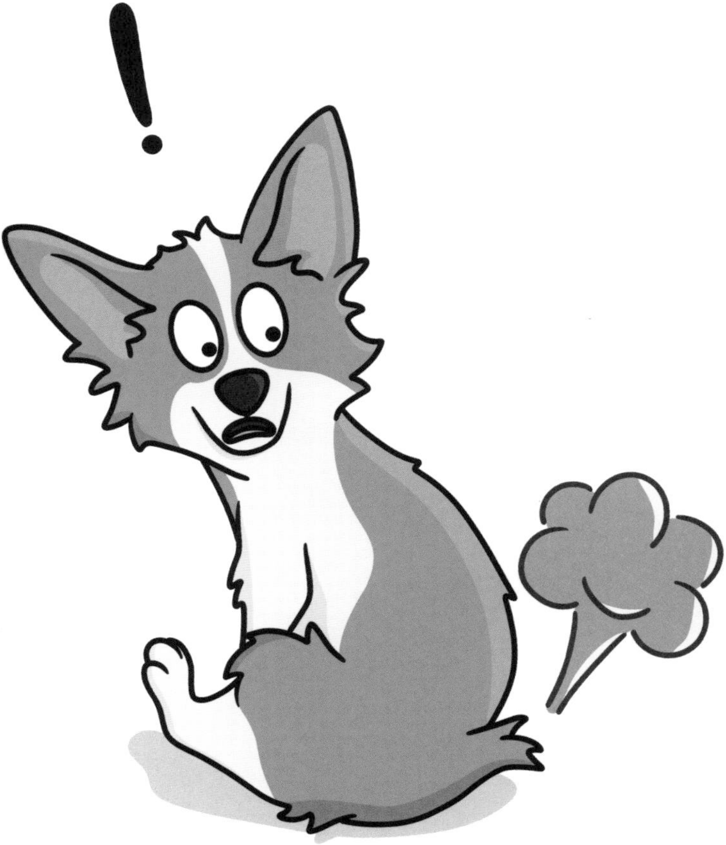

Your dog will love
the new squeaky toy you
bought. And will show their
appreciation by playing
with it at 3 a.m.

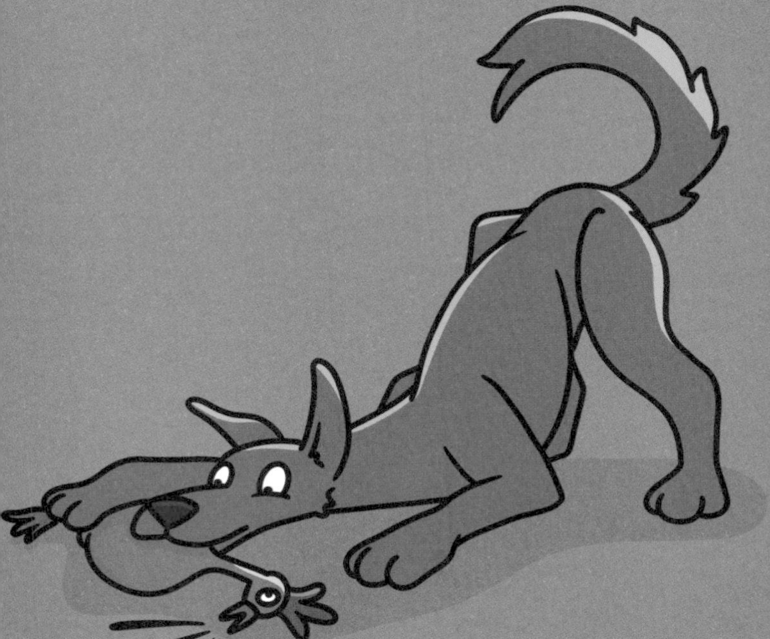

Get ready to embrace
a new fashion trend:
paw-print fabric.

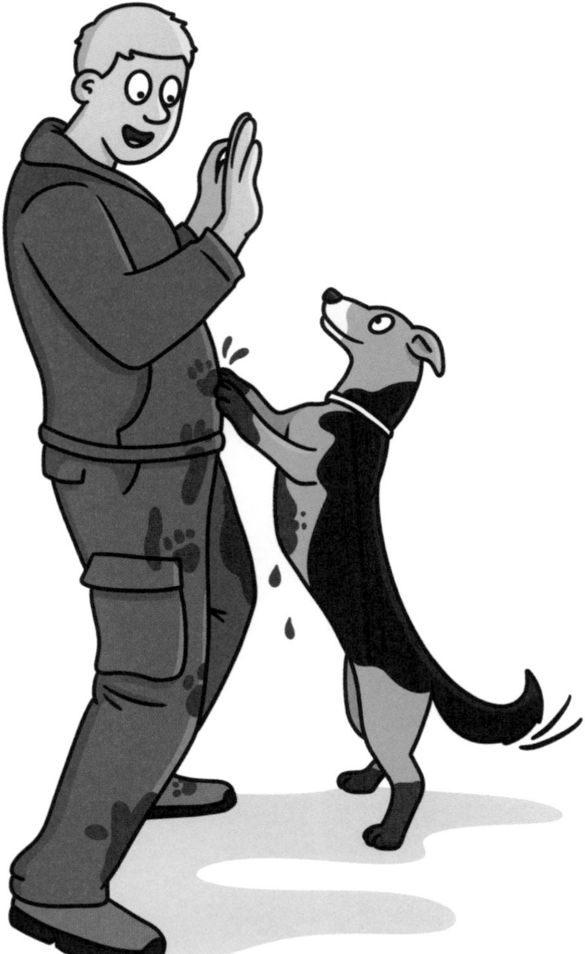

Always allow extra
time to arrive at your
destination. Your dog
will need to investigate
a lot along the way.

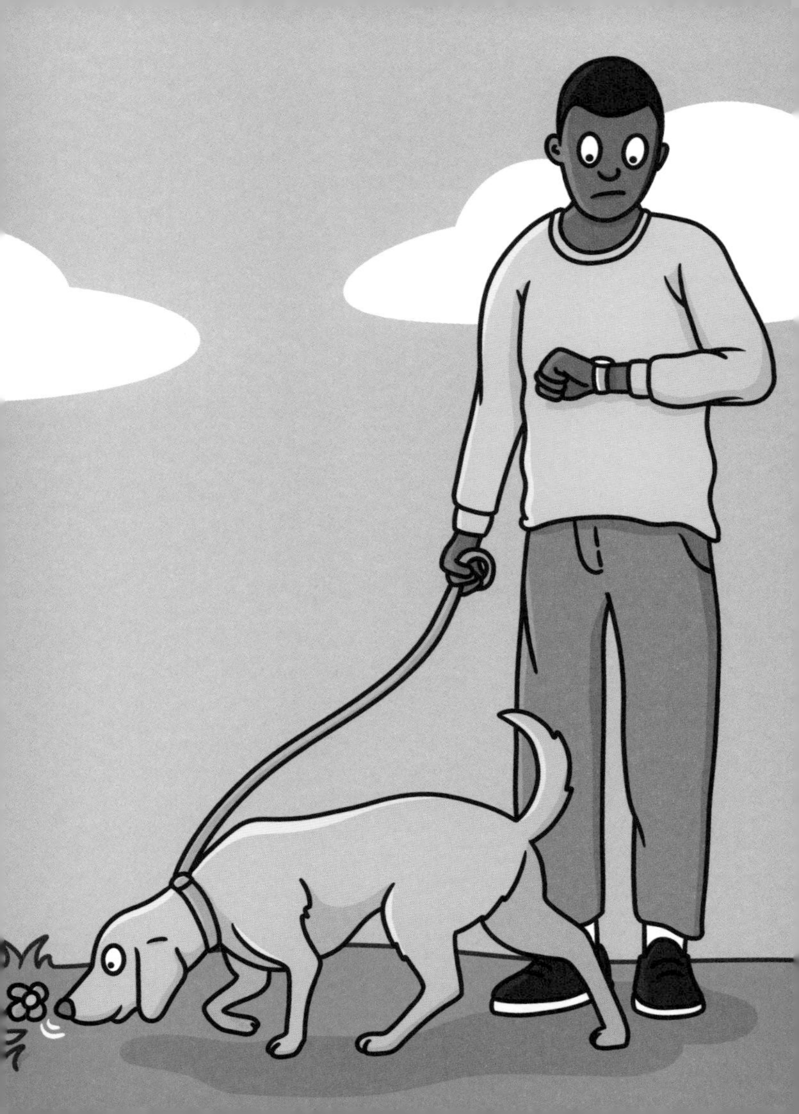

When it comes to tidying up cluttered surfaces, your dog will be happy to help out.

Keep your toilet lid closed at all times. Unless you don't mind it becoming the local drinking hole.

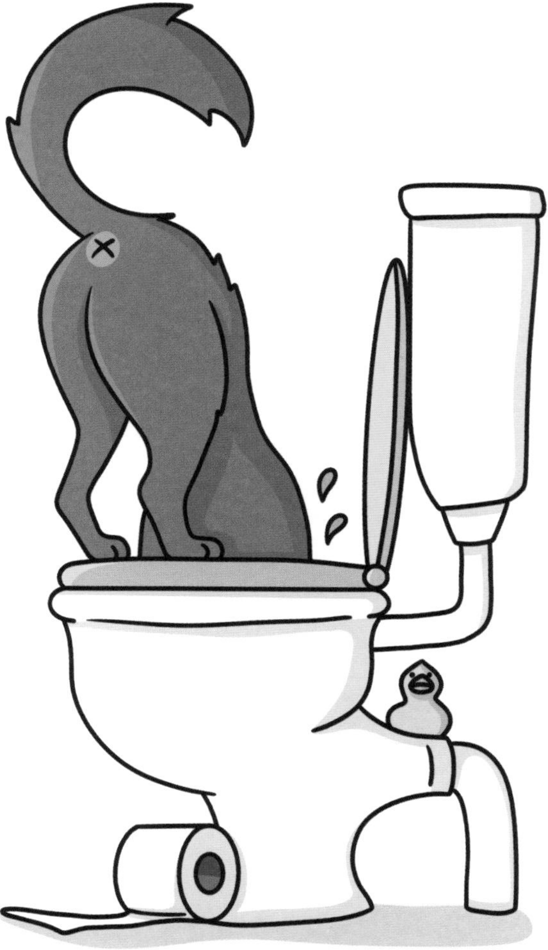

Dogs are gymnastic animals. They have even mastered the art of standing on three legs.

Whoever arrives at
your house will be
greeted with a gift.

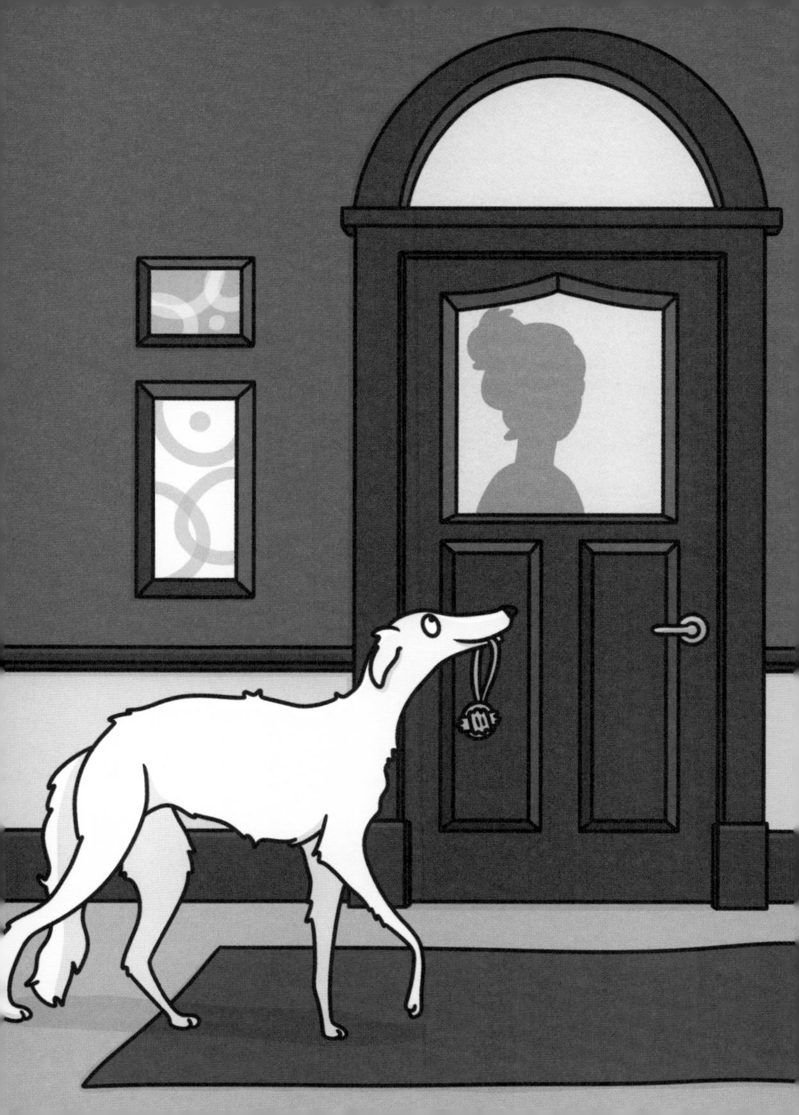

The amount of space required for your dog to sleep comfortably is twice the area of their body, plus half of the area of your body, plus extra for margins.

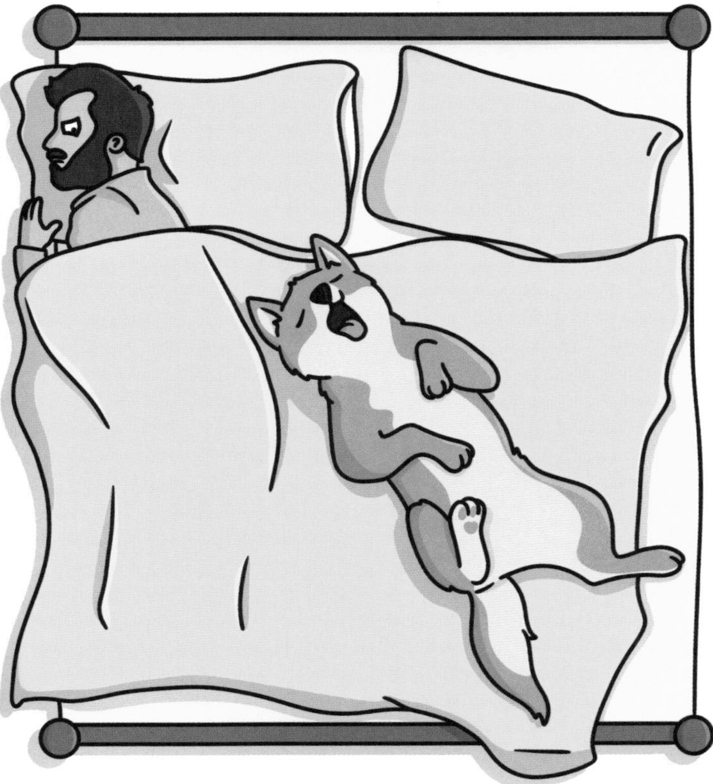

Your dog can tell when
you're feeling too hot
and a refreshing shower
would be in order.

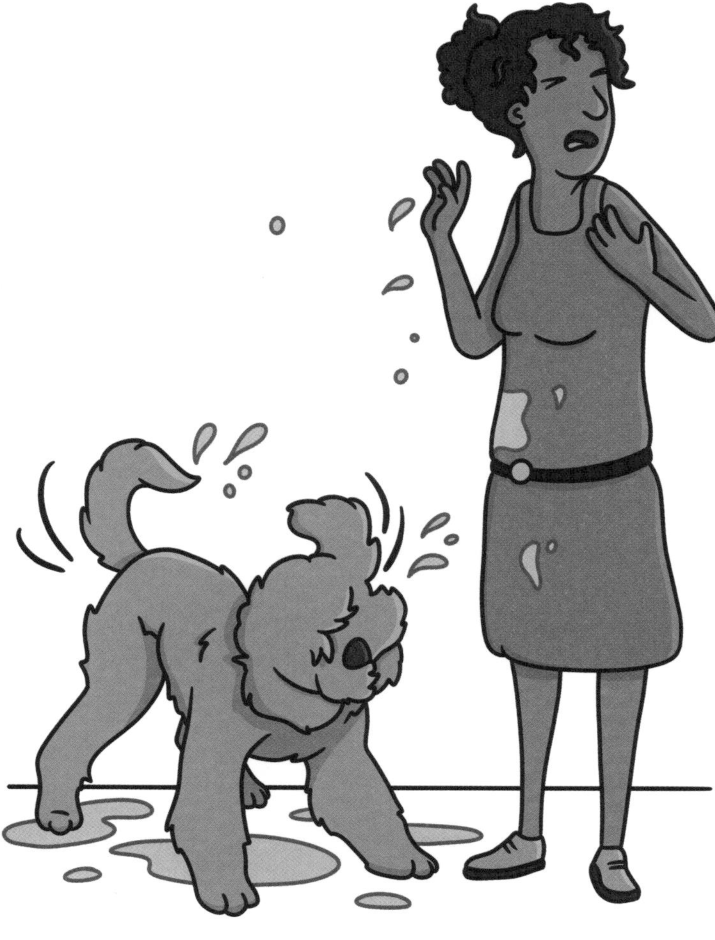

Food should not
be left unsupervised
at any time.

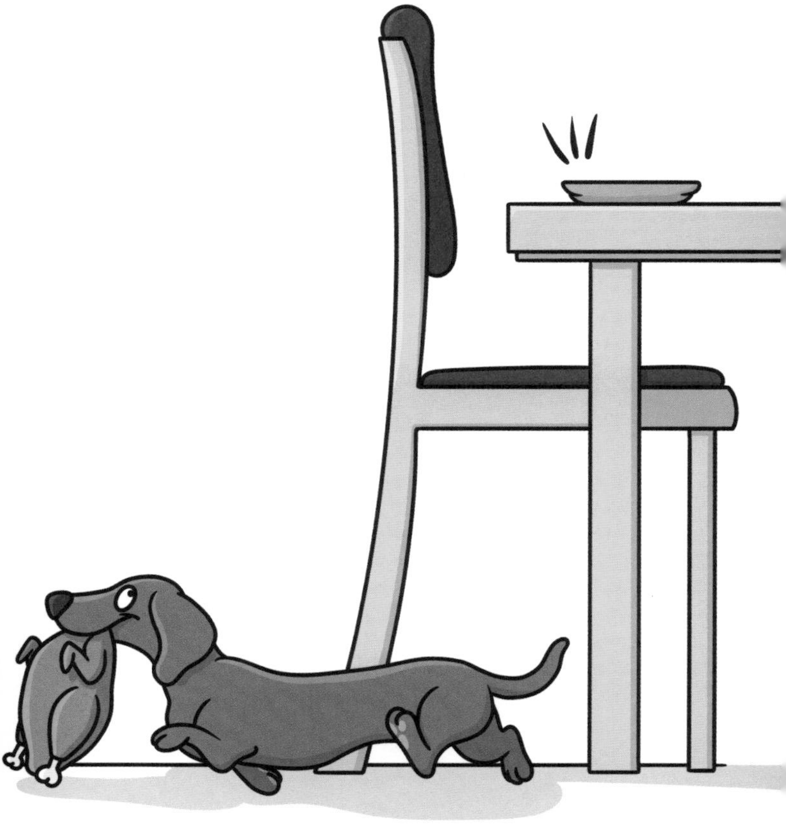

It is important that your dog has access to fresh air on car journeys.

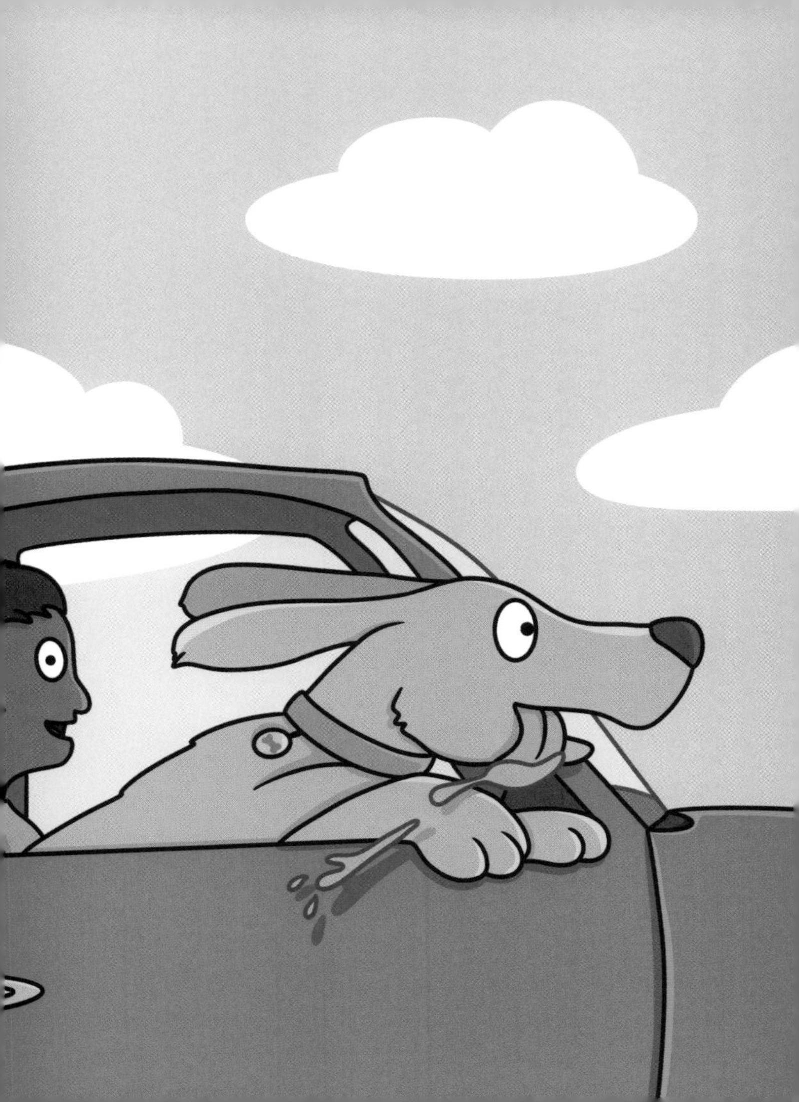

Providing your dog with entertainment will help to keep their brain sharp.

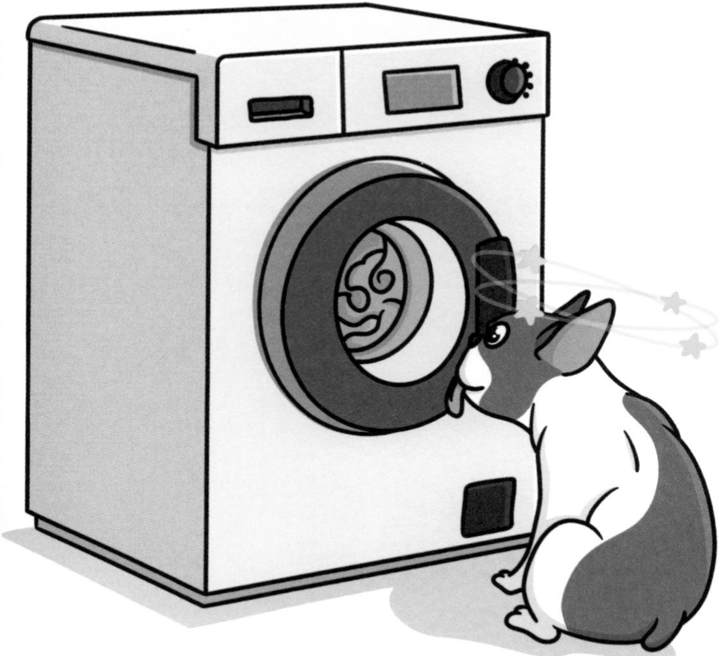

As a dog parent, you can expect your flexibility to increase impressively.

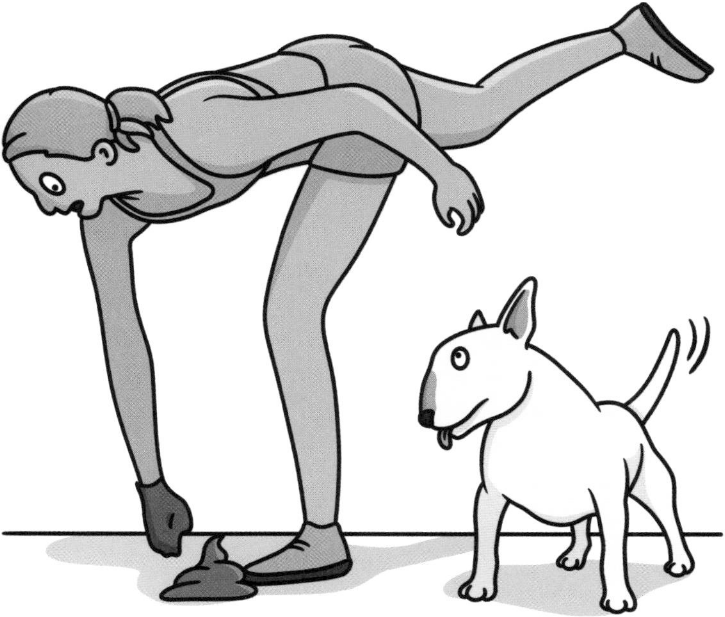

The bigger the stick,
the better.

It is important to supply your furry friend with the most comfortable dog bed on the market. Just don't expect them to sleep in it.

Having a dog will
help you to cut down
on dishwashing costs.

As a dog parent,
you can only guess
at what your pooch
might be dreaming.

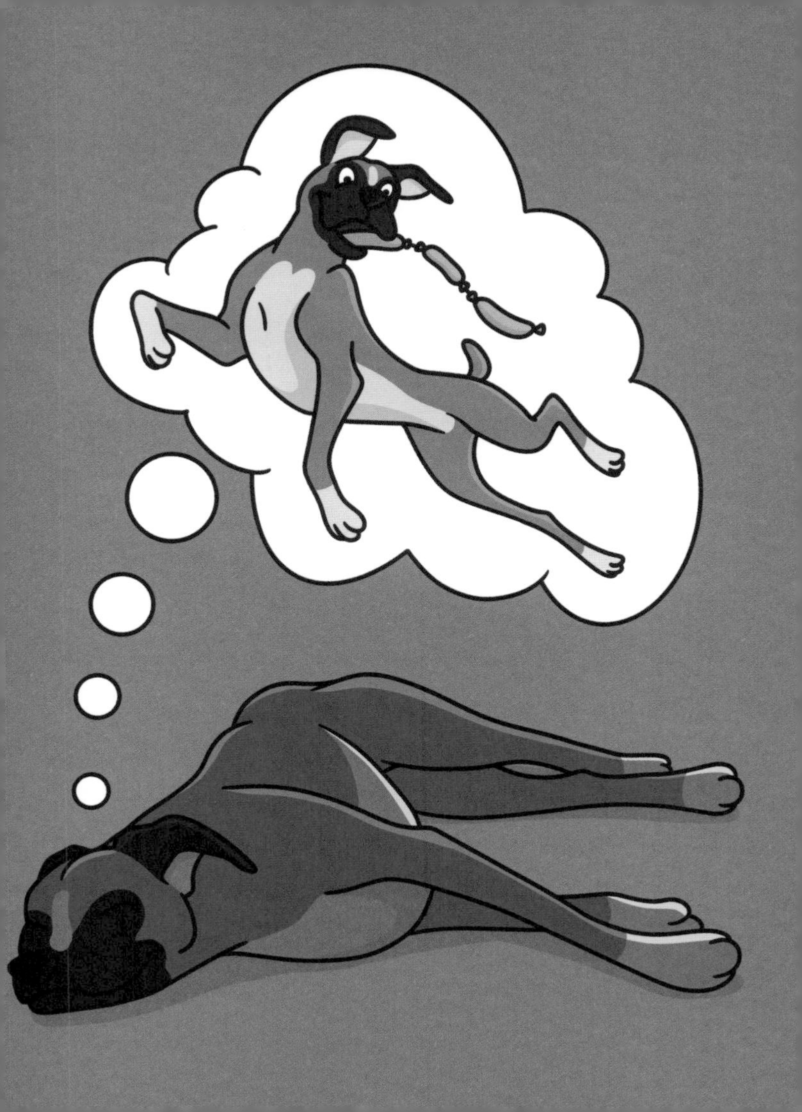

If your dog bestows
the sacred greeting of
their people upon you,
take it as a compliment.

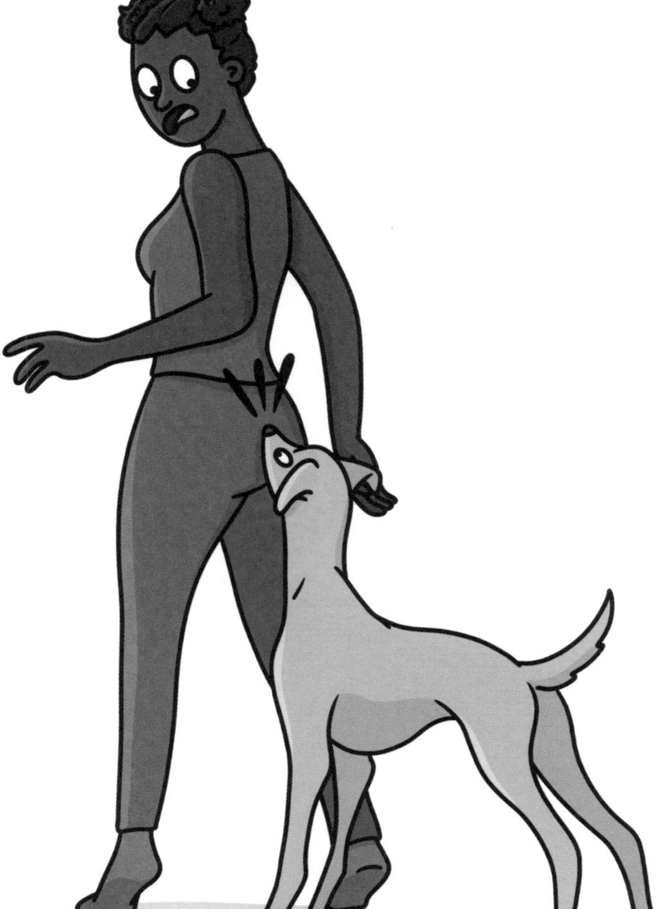

If you leave your dog
alone at home, don't
be surprised if you
come back to find
they have rearranged
things somewhat.

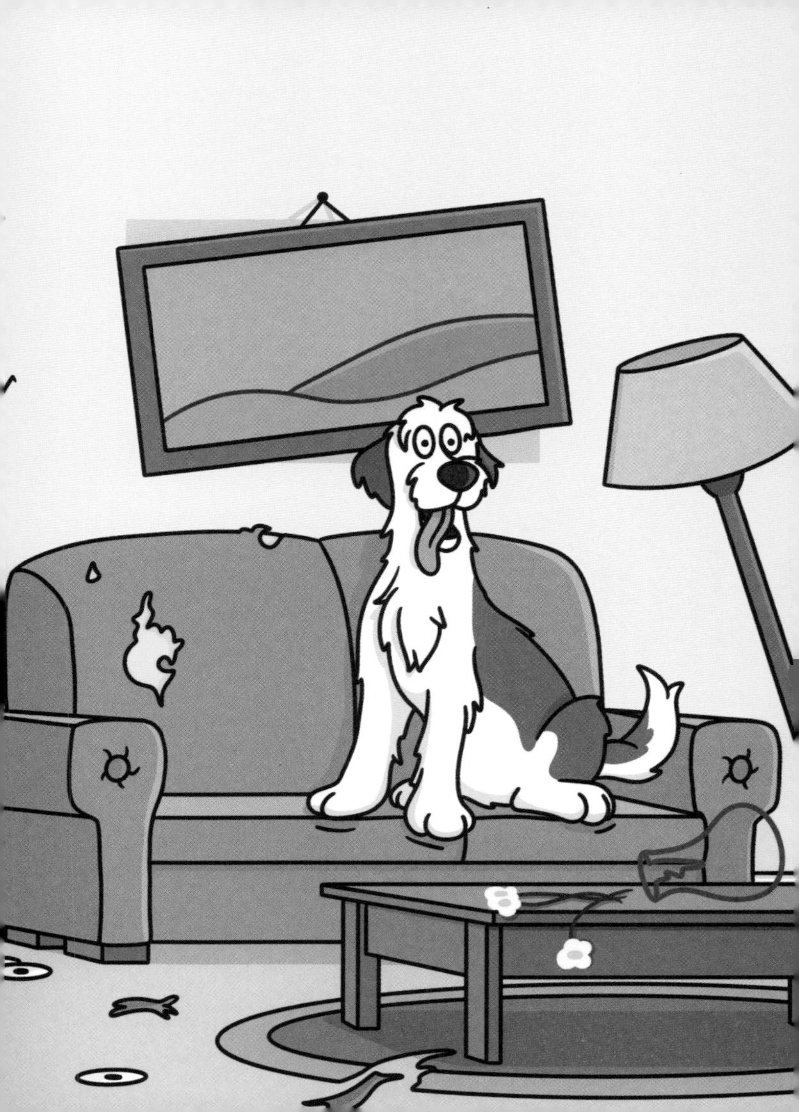

Your dog may have eccentric tastes when it comes to amorous partners, and that's okay. Love is love!

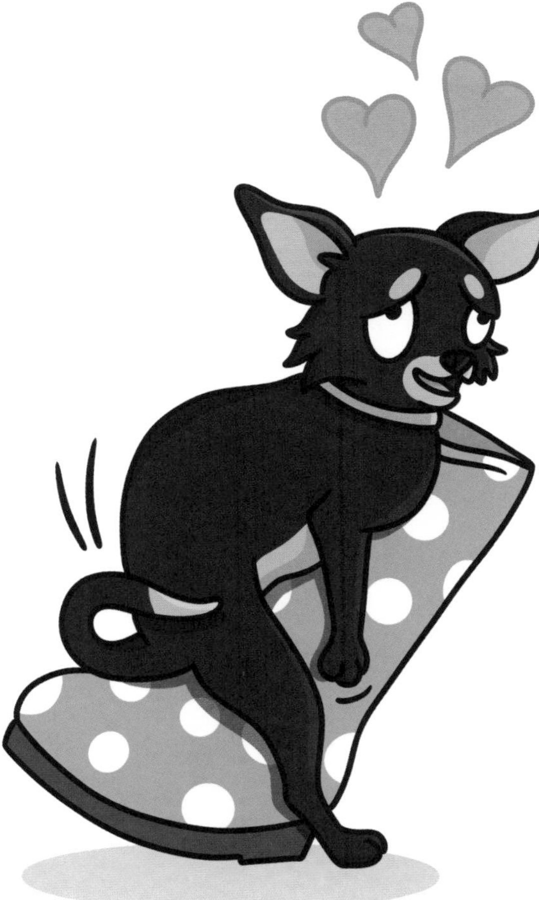

Your dog will alert
you immediately should
they detect any threats
to your safety while
out on your walk.

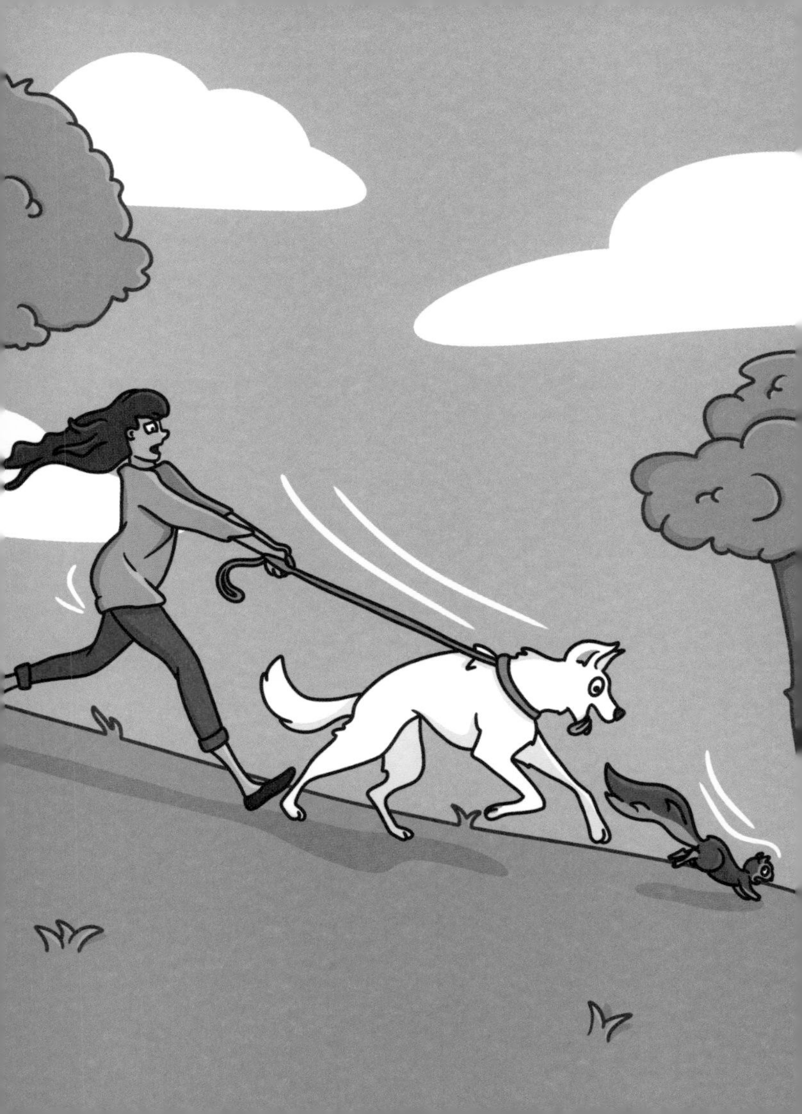

Dogs are masters of
self-entertainment.

Bicycles are to
be treated with the
utmost suspicion.

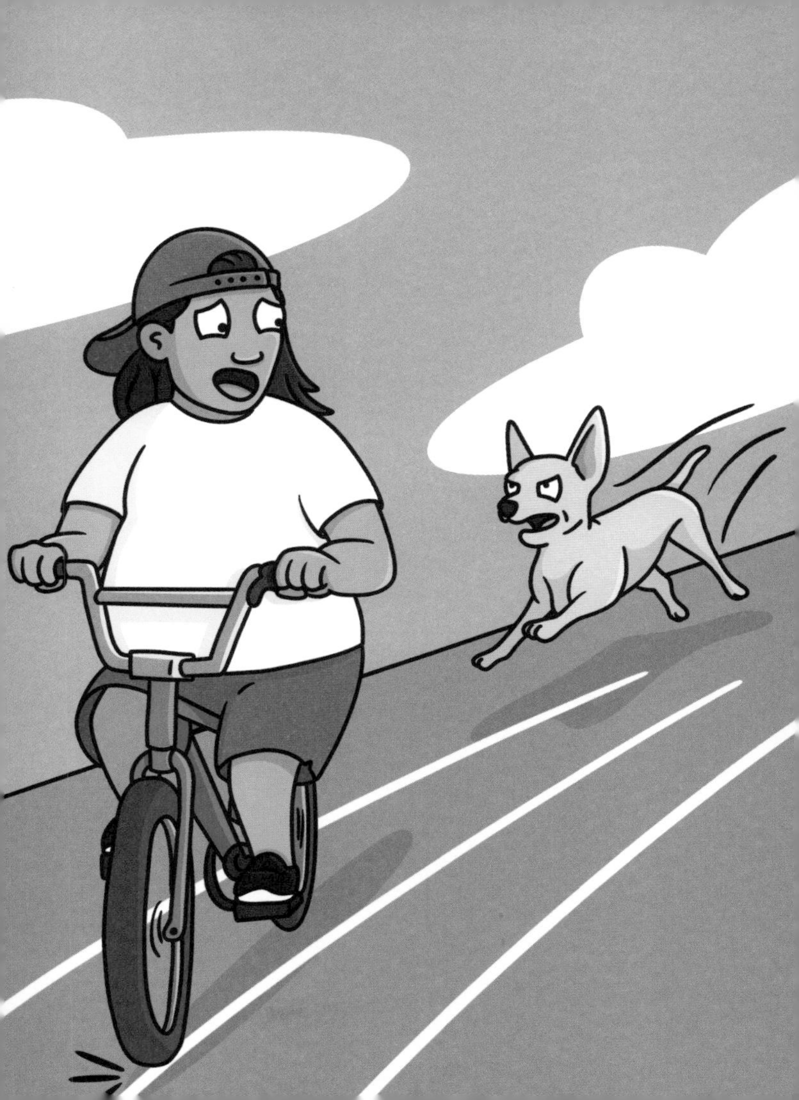

A little-known
fact about dogs:
they are accomplished
maypole dancers.

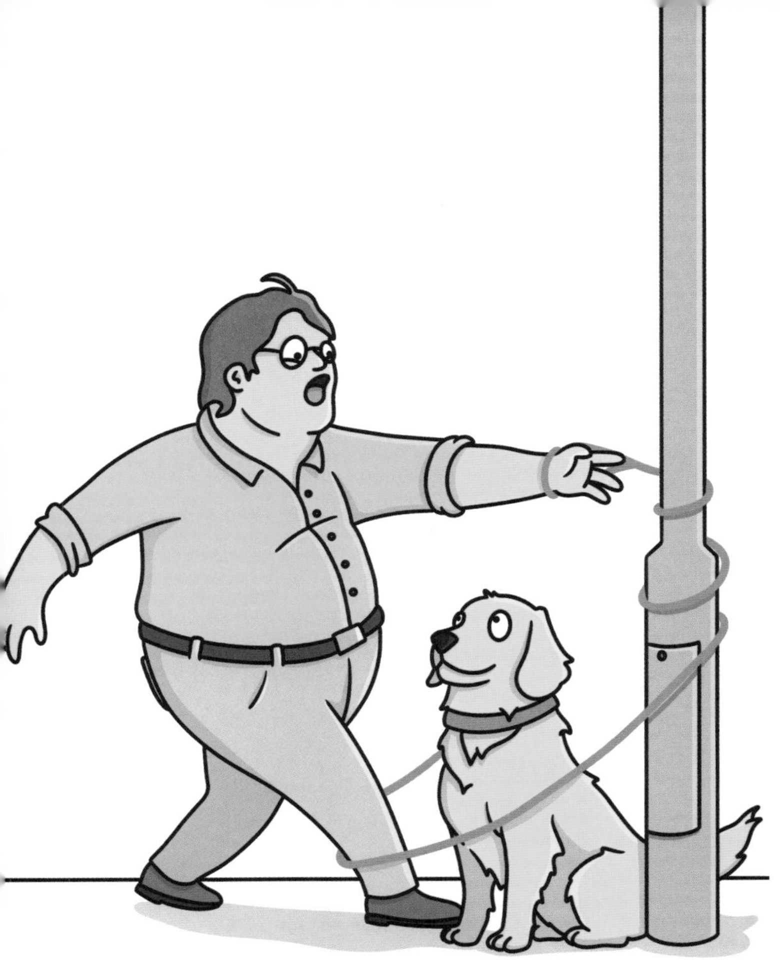

Please note: at the time of writing, the ongoing conflict between caninekind and their arch enemy, The Postie, shows no sign of abating.

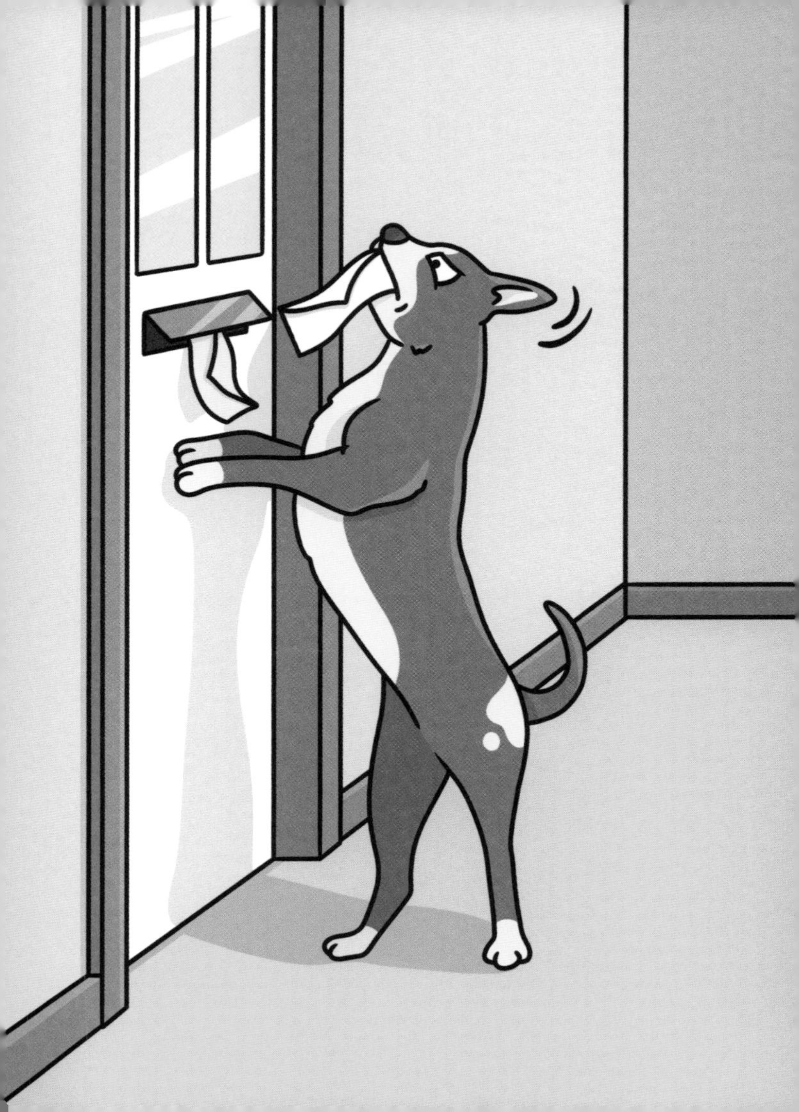

No matter how many times you try to throw that old tennis ball away, your dog will always bring it back.

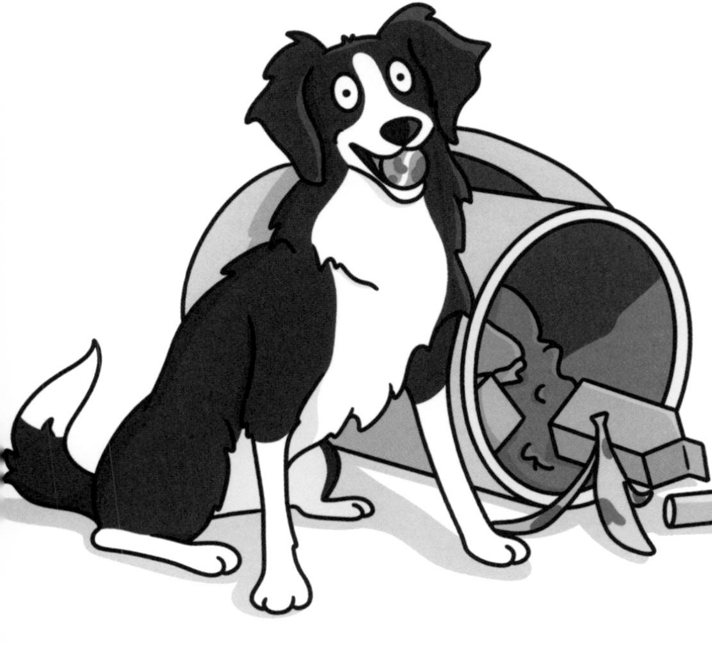

You can count on
your dog to help out
in the garden.

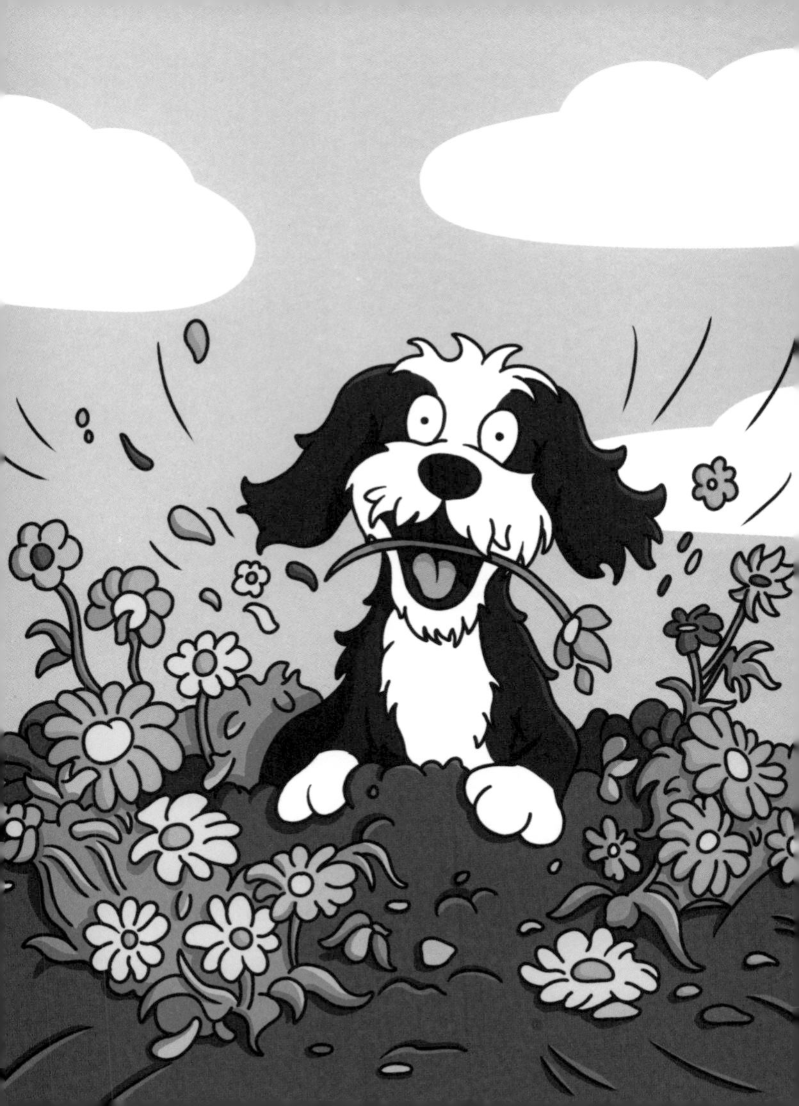

Your dog takes their role as home security very seriously and will keep tabs on where you are. At all times.

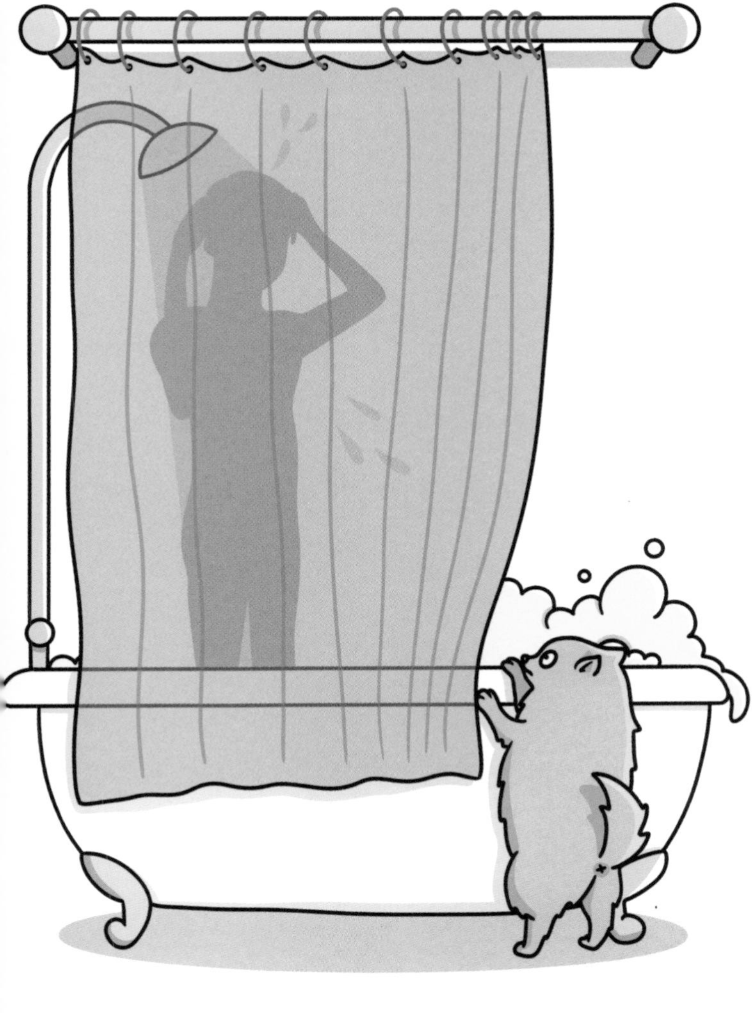

Sprinklers were
invented purely for the
amusement of dogs.

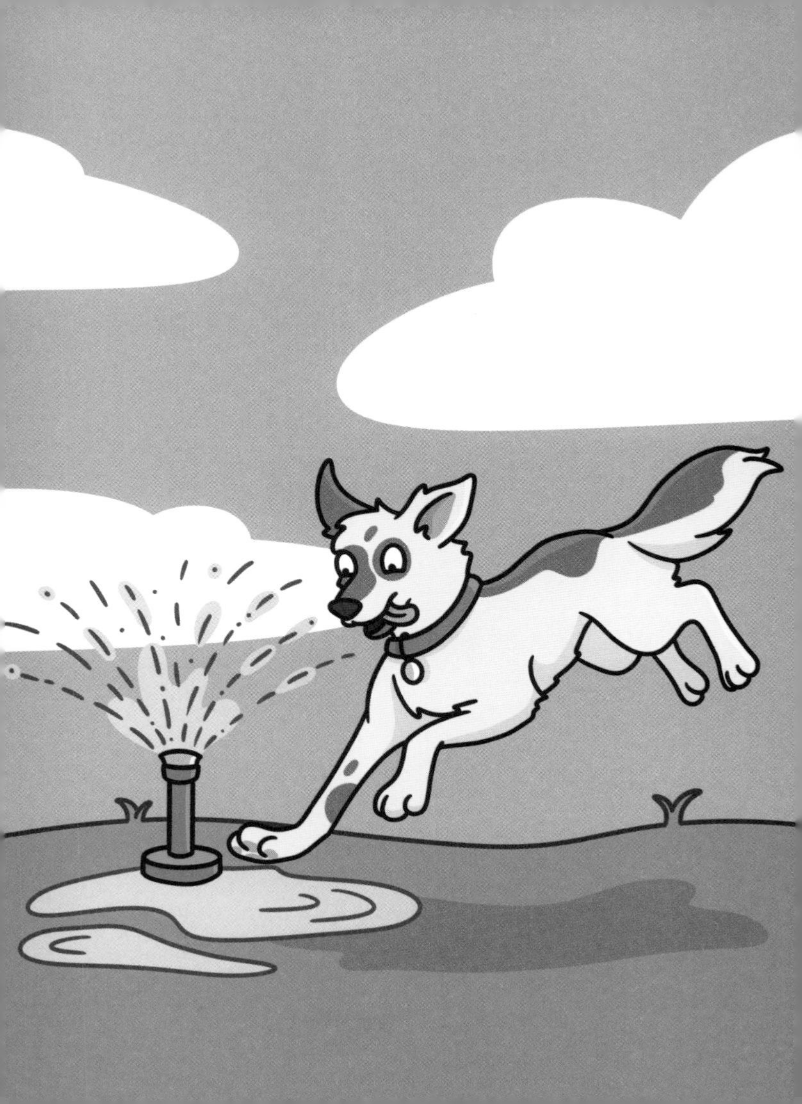

Dogs love nothing more than a good old scrub. A weekly bath will help keep your soft furnishings clean!

Want to know where
all your odd socks and
the remote control are?
Ask your dog.

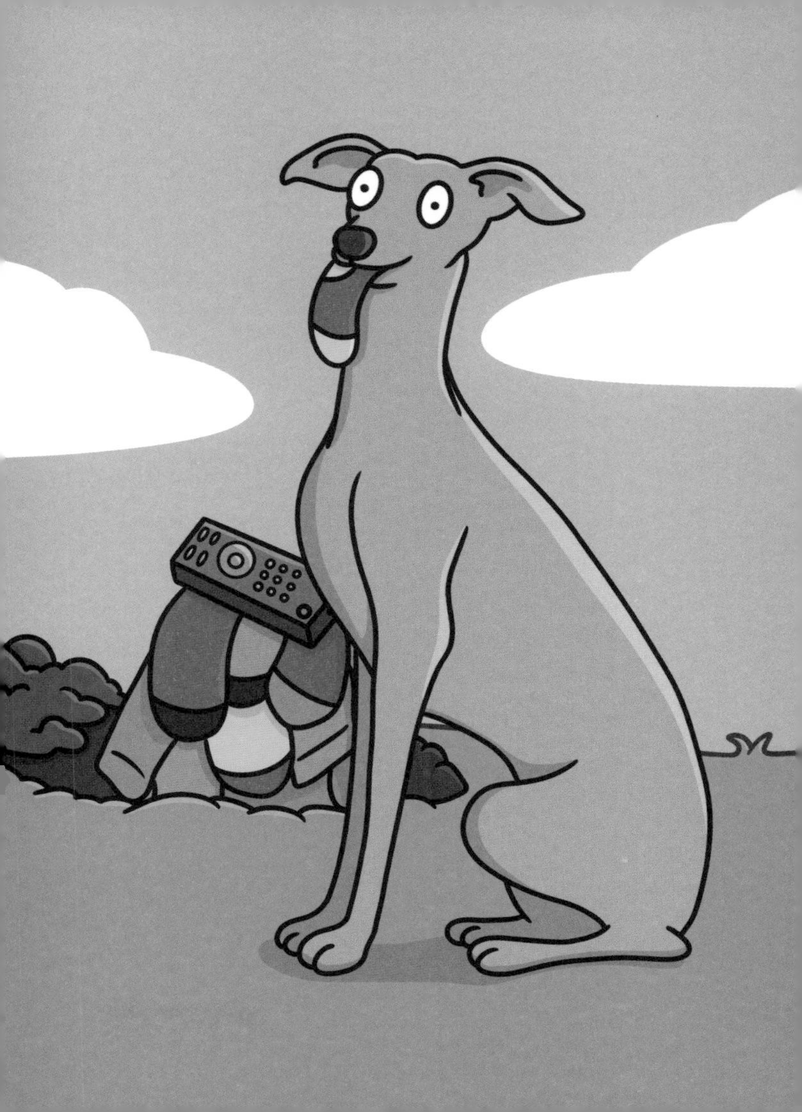

It's called the zoomies and no one knows quite why it happens. Not even your dog.

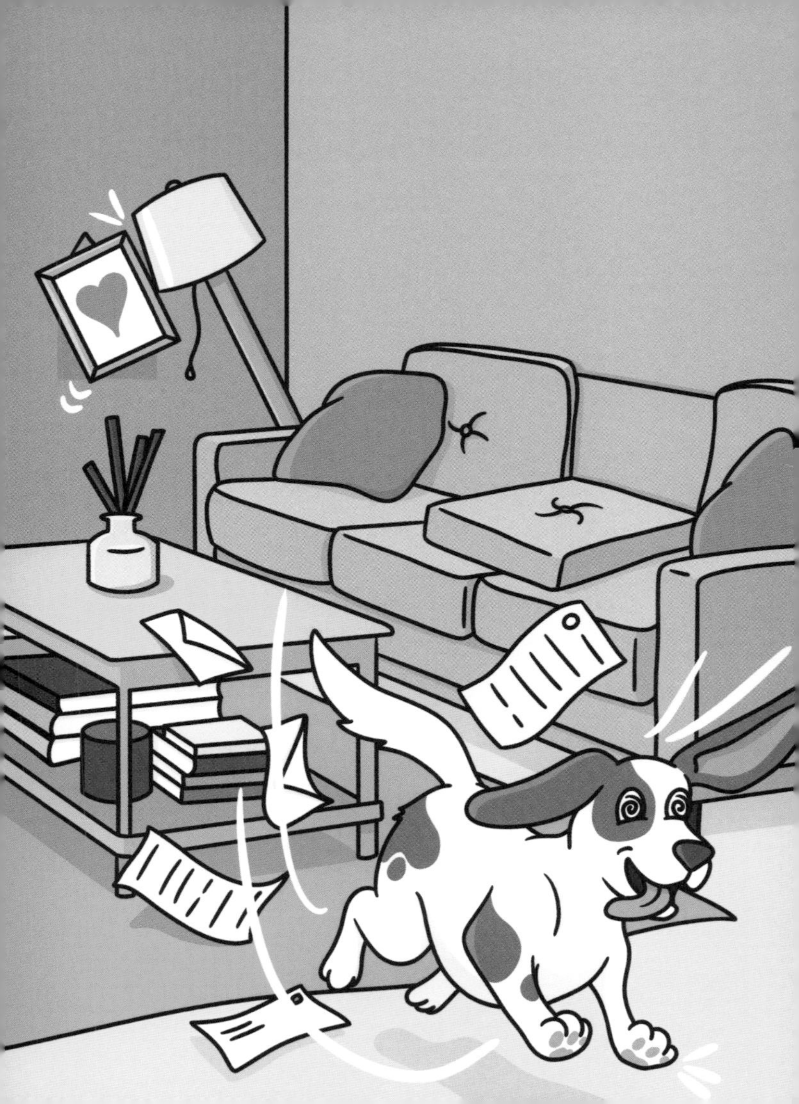

Above all, nothing compares to the joy of that hero's welcome when you come home after a long day.

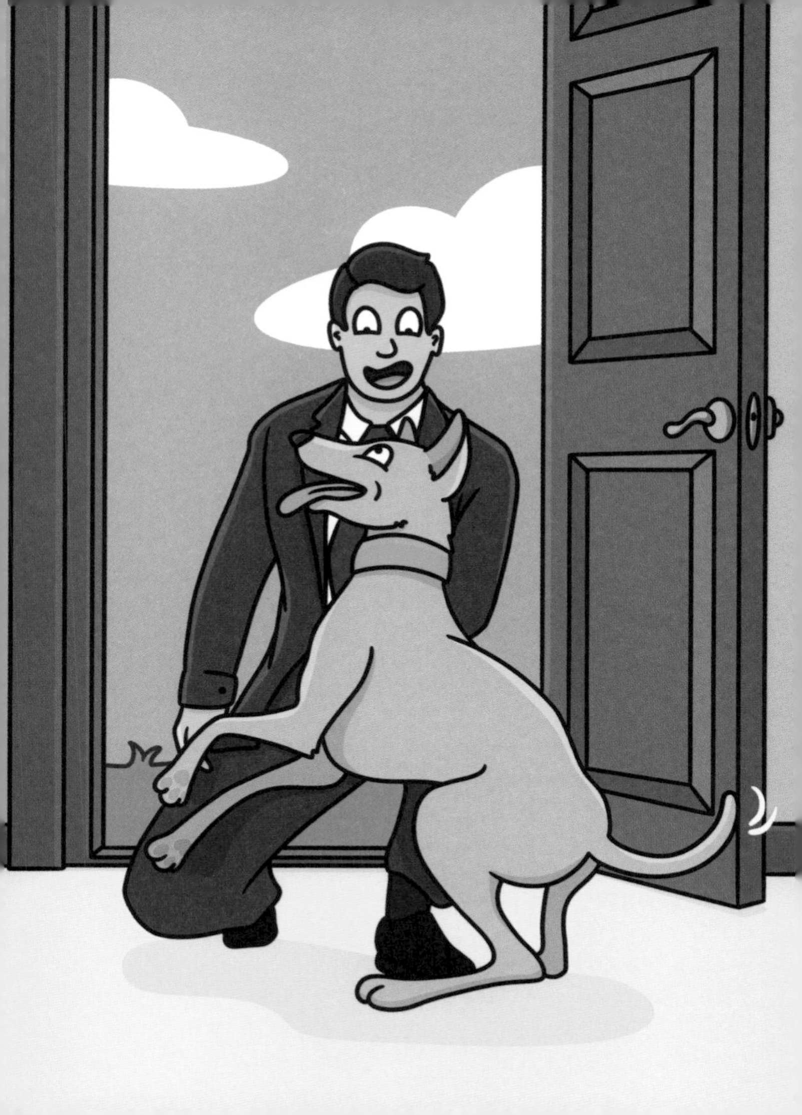

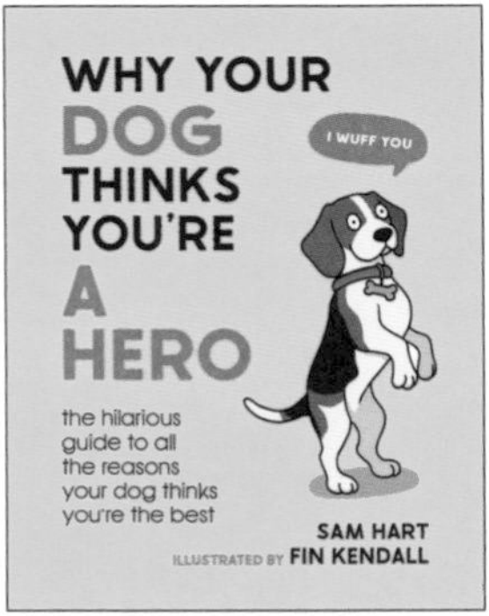
WHY YOUR DOG THINKS YOU'RE A HERO
I WUFF YOU
the hilarious guide to all the reasons your dog thinks you're the best
SAM HART
ILLUSTRATED BY FIN KENDALL

Why Your Dog Thinks You're A Hero

Written by Sam Hart
Illustrated by Fin Kendall

978-1-80007-931-1

This hilarious and heartfelt gift book is the perfect guide to the many reasons why your dog thinks you are a hero

Owning a dog is to have a four-legged best friend who worships your every move. Each time you walk through the door, you become the centre of their universe, and their love for you is only matched by their love of scoffing sausages and chasing cats. As their amazing owner, you know what it takes to care for them, but allow this book to show how much it means to your furry friend.

THE
DOG OWNER'S
SURVIVAL GUIDE
SOPHIE JOHNSON
ILLUSTRATED BY TATIANA DAVIDOVA

The Dog Owner's Survival Guide

Written by Sophie Johnson
Illustrated by Tatiana Davidova

978-1-80007-400-2

A hilarious, fully illustrated book full of tongue-in-cheek advice for surviving life as a dog parent – the perfect gift for any dog lover

This no-nonsense guide is here to teach you all the tricks you'll ever need to help you navigate life with your furry friend, so you can focus on the positives – like giving them head-scritches and nose-boops every time they prove they're a good doggo at heart.

Have you enjoyed this book?
If so, find us on Facebook
at Summersdale Publishers, on
Twitter/X at @Summersdale
and on Instagram and TikTok
at @summersdalebooks
and get in touch.
We'd love to hear from you!

www.summersdale.com